WILD ABOUT SNAKES

GARTER SNAKES

BY HEATHER L. MONTGOMERY

Consultant:
Robert Mason, PhD
Professor of Zoology
J.C. Braly Curator of Vertebrates
Oregon State University, Corvallis

CAPSTONE PRESS
a capstone imprint

Edge Books are published by Capstone Press,
151 Good Counsel Drive, P.O. Box 669, Mankato, Minnesota 56002.
www.capstonepub.com

Books published by Capstone Press are manufactured with paper
containing at least 10 percent post-consumer waste.

Library of Congress Cataloging-in-Publication Data
Montgomery, Heather L.
  Garter snakes / by Heather Montgomery.
    p. cm.—(Edge books. Wild about snakes)
  Includes bibliographical references and index.
  Summary: "Describes garter snakes including their distinctive
characteristics, habitats, and defenses"—Provided by publisher.
  ISBN 978-1-4296-5433-3 (library binding)
  ISBN 978-1-4296-6257-4 (paperback)
  1. Garter snakes—Juvenile literature. I. Title. II. Series.
QL666.O636M645 2011
597.96'2—dc22   2010025208

Editorial Credits
Kathryn Clay and Anthony Wacholtz, editors; Kyle Grenz, designer;
    Eric Gohl, media researcher; Eric Manske, production specialist

Photo Credits
Alamy/All Canada Photos, 20; Kevin Ebi, 25
AP Images/Edmund D. Brodie, Jr., 13 (right)
BigStockPhoto.com/Otis Galleries, 12–13; Pixart, 26–27; Steve Byland, 10
Dreamstime/Jason Poston, 7; Steve Byland, 14–15
iStockphoto/Stephen Goodwin, 4–5
Landov LLC/Reuters/Fred Greenslade, 28–29
Newscom, 22–23
Photo Researchers, Inc/Cosmos Blank, 19
Shutterstock/Eric Rounds, 16–17; Gerald A. DeBoer, cover; Jason Mintzer, 1;
    Lorraine Swanson, 23 (right); malko, 9 (person silhouette); Marilyn Volan,
    background; Paunovic, 9 (snake silhouette)
Wikipedia/Dave Feliz, 8; Public Domain, 5 (right)

Printed in the United States of America in Stevens Point, Wisconsin.

TABLE OF CONTENTS

Chapter 1

SPOTTING A GARTER SNAKE

You're strolling along a riverbank, looking for a good place to fish. Something moves in the weeds in front of you. Your heartbeat quickens as you suck in a deep breath. You sneak forward to see what it is. A thin snake slips between blades of grass and slithers away from you. The yellow stripes running the length of its body tell you this small **reptile** is a garter snake.

reptile—a cold-blooded animal that breathes air and has a backbone; most reptiles lay eggs and have scaly skin

What's in a Name?

A garter is a type of clothing that used to hold up socks. Garters were made from long, colorful ribbons. Garter snakes got their name because the long stripes on their bodies look like the ribbons on a garter. Garter snakes have also been called ribbon snakes.

Uncommonly Common

Thirty different **species** of garter snakes are found throughout North America. Like all reptiles, garter snakes are **cold-blooded**. Their body temperature matches the temperature of the air and ground around them. But unlike other snakes, garter snakes can survive in cold temperatures. Some garter snakes can also live as far south as Mexico.

Almost all garter snakes live near water. Some, like the common garter, can live just about anywhere. Others prefer a single habitat like a grassy meadow, shallow pond, or stream bank.

species—a specific type of animal or plant
cold-blooded—having a body temperature that

Garter Snake Range

☐ where garter snakes live

Asia

North
America

Europe

Africa

N
W ⊕ E
S

South
America

Australia

Antarctica

Female garter snakes are larger than males. Their bodies must be large to hold their babies.

Size and Lifespan

Most garter snakes have black or brown scales with yellow, white, orange, or red stripes. These small snakes are about 2 to 3 feet (0.6 to 0.9 meter) long. The giant garter snake can grow to more than 4 feet (1.2 meters) long.

Garter snakes never stop growing. Every year their bones add rings like the rings on a tree. Scientists tell the age of a garter snake by looking at the rings in its tailbone. In the wild, garter snakes live about 10 to 15 years.

Garter snakes are common pets because they are not **venomous**. Their small size makes them easy to handle. When raised as pets, garter snakes can become gentle and dependent on people. In captivity they may live up to 22 years.

The average height of an American male is 5 feet, 10 inches (178 centimeters)

venomous—able to produce a toxic substance

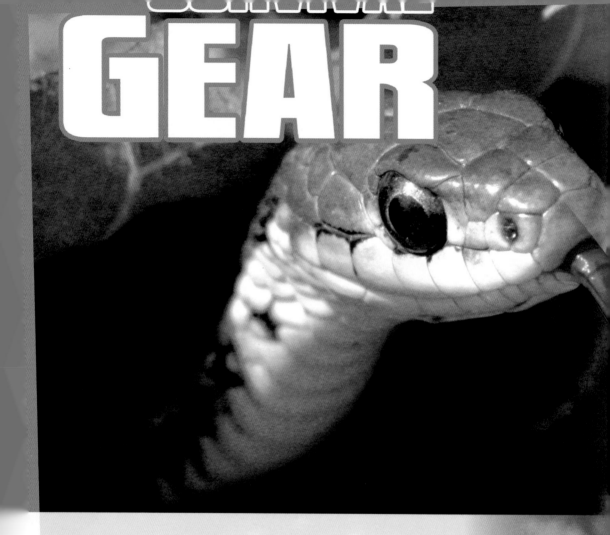

GEAR

From the moment a garter snake wakes up, it has to be alert. Special adaptations, such as a sharp sense of sight and smell, help keep the snake alive. These unique senses also help the garter snake be a successful hunter.

Sensational Senses

If you look a garter snake in the eyes, you will notice it has large, round pupils. Although it cannot see in the dark, a garter snake sees extremely well in the daytime. Its eyes are designed to see the tiny movements of its **prey**.

If a **predator** sneaks up from behind, garter snakes need to be prepared. Garter snakes lack ears and can't hear approaching enemies. But they do have ear bones. A snake's ear bones are connected to its jawbones. The jawbones rest on the ground. When the ground shakes, the jaw wiggles and the ear bones vibrate. The ear bones allow a garter snake to sense approaching enemies.

A garter snake doesn't use its tongue for tasting. Garter snakes flick their tongues in and out to pick up smells floating in the air. The smells are placed on the roof of the snake's mouth. The smells activate a sensitive area called the Jacobson's organ. It helps the snake identify prey.

prey—an animal hunted by another animal for food
predator—an animal that hunts other animals for food

11

Dinner Time

A garter's favorite food depends on the species. Just like people, some snakes are picky eaters. The Pacific coast aquatic garter snake hangs out by the water and eats fish, frogs, and salamanders. Butler's garter snakes prefer worms and slugs. The checkered garter isn't picky at all. It will eat frogs, earthworms, lizards, fish, and dead animals. Some garter snakes also eat insects, crawfish, small birds, or mice.

Newts for Dinner

Rough-skinned newts carry a poison in their skin. Some common garter snakes are the only animals that can eat them. The newts' poison doesn't harm these predators.

Over many years, the newts began producing more poison to keep away enemies. A single rough-skinned newt now carries enough poison to kill 10 people. But garter snakes adapted to the large amount of poison.

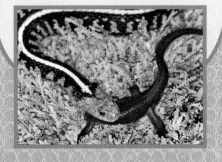

Handling a pet garter snake shortly after it eats may make it throw up its meal.

13

On the Prowl

Most garters search for their food.
They don't wait for food to come to them.
A hungry garter snake might slither through
the reeds. Moving along the edge of a pond,
it flicks its tongue in and out.

When it sees prey nearby, the snake silently moves toward it. The prey may try to escape, but the snake closes in. The prey freezes, and for a moment the snake loses track of the small animal. When the prey thinks things are safe, it settles down in the mud. This is when the snake strikes, grabbing the animal with its tiny teeth. As the prey struggles, the snake coats it with saliva. Special **enzymes** in a garter snake's saliva can stun prey.

Big Mouth

Some garter snakes loop their bodies around their prey to hold the animals in place. Then they turn the prey so that it will go down headfirst. Doing so makes the prey slide down smoothly through the throat without getting its legs and feet caught.

When eating very large prey, a garter snake may bite on it for a while. The biting allows the enzymes in the snake's saliva to start breaking down the food. Next, the jaws begin the process of swallowing the food. The left side of the jaw slides forward and sinks in. The right side follows. Then the process repeats itself. The snake's jaws, skull, and skin stretch to reach around the food.

Every time a red-sided garter snake eats,
its small intestine and liver grow. After
the food has been digested, the organs
shrink back to their original size.

Chapter 3

CHANGING WITH THE SEASONS

A garter snake chooses its home based on the air temperature, food availability, and types of shelter nearby. To handle the challenges in its environment, a garter snake follows a yearly routine. The schedule helps the snake grow, have young, and survive during changing seasons.

Summertime

When the weather is warm, a garter snake grows. As the snake grows, its skin becomes too small and needs to shed. To shed its skin, the snake rubs its chin against a rock. The old skin splits near the mouth. This is when things get tough. The snake finds a stick to hook the old skin and help pull it off. After about an hour of struggling, the snake slithers away in its new skin.

Young snakes are constantly growing and may shed four to five times a year. Adult snakes may shed only a couple times each year.

Sometimes patches of old scales stick to the snake. If this happens to the scales over the eye, the snake can become blind.

Hibernation Hideout

Because garter snakes are cold-blooded, they can't make their own body heat. They warm their bodies with heat from the sun, water, rocks, and ground. Garter snakes prefer to keep their bodies between 82 and 89 degrees Fahrenheit (28 and 32 degrees Celsius). For this reason, they are most active during the warm daytime hours.

When the weather cools off in the fall, their lifestyle has to change. Unlike most snakes, garter snakes can live in colder climates. But in order to survive the winter, they must seek shelter. Many species **hibernate** from October to March. They slip into animal dens, tree stumps, rock piles, or small caves to find a warm spot. Some snakes hibernate in nearby areas. Others **migrate** up to 20 miles (32 kilometers) to find the perfect spot. Sometimes tens of thousands of snakes share a single den for a long winter nap.

hibernate—to spend winter in a resting state to survive poor conditions in the environment

migrate—to move from one place to another when seasons change or when food is scarce

21

Spring Fever

In spring garter snakes become active. The males come out of their shelters first and wait for the females. Though hungry, the males won't start hunting until they have mated. Like someone wearing perfume, a female garter snake leaves a scent behind her. The males follow the scent to track her down. Hundreds of males may be attracted to one female. They climb on each other, creating a pile the size of a beach ball. Sometimes the female is crushed under all the weight.

While most snakes lay eggs, garter snakes do not. Instead, the mothers carry the young inside their bodies. In the late summer or early fall, they give birth to 10 to 20 babies. Some garter snake species have up to 50 babies at one time.

Snake Crossing

Every fall, red-sided garter snakes head to the Narcisse Snake Dens in Manitoba, Canada, for hibernation. In this part of Canada, the ground freezes 10 feet (3 meters) deep in the winter. Shelters for hibernation can be hard to find. But red-sided garters have discovered sinkholes that they return to year after year. Thousands of snakes heap together into a few deep sinkholes. When they come out of the holes in spring, the ground looks like a river of snakes.

The snakes must cross busy roads to get to the sinkholes. In the past, many snakes were crushed by cars. To protect the snakes, people built tunnels under the roads. Fences guide the snakes into the tunnels. Road signs remind drivers to slow down. Now, many more snakes make it to their crowded dens.

Chapter 4

DANGERS TO GARTER SNAKES

For a garter snake, life in the wild is dangerous. Raccoons, foxes, hawks, turtles, fish, and even cats hunt garter snakes. Survival is especially tough for baby garters. Only 20 percent of red-sided garter snakes survive their first year. The small snakes make an easy dinner for predators.

Harmful Humans

People can be especially harmful to garter snakes. Humans move in and take over garter snakes' habitats. They run over snakes slithering across roads. Some people collect wild garter snakes to sell as pets. Captive snakes are not always fed the right food or kept at an appropriate temperature. Many captive snakes die.

Total Trickster

Unlike young snakes, adult garters can outsmart some enemies. When threatened, a garter snake first tries to sneak away or dive underwater. A garter would rather not fight. If it is cornered, it uses a number of tricks.

Some garters fool their enemies by widening their bodies to look bigger. Flattening their heads, they can look like a venomous snake. Others may act mean and strike. Even then, they might not bite. Sometimes they strike without even opening their mouth. These fake moves often scare away an enemy.

If a garter snake is picked up, the predator should watch out! The snake will squirt a slippery, smelly liquid called musk from under its tail. The snake may also poop. Twisting in the predator's grip, the garter snake will smear a stinky mix all over it. The predator will probably drop the snake. Some garter snakes, especially pregnant ones, will play dead when picked up.

When attacked, a western plains garter may roll into a ball and hide its head. It wiggles its tail to trick its enemy into attacking that end instead of the head.

Garter with a Narrow Head

Narrow-headed garters love the water. They can be found in streams in Arizona, New Mexico, and parts of Mexico. Because these snakes spend so much time in the water, scientists once thought they were water snakes. And unlike other garter snakes, narrow-headed garters don't have stripes. They are gray-brown with dark spots.

While most garter snakes are common, narrow-headed garters are becoming rare. Crayfish have moved in from other areas. They often eat the young snakes. They also eat the snakes' main food sources.

Erosion can also be a problem for narrow-headed garters. Dirt washing into streams fills in the snakes' fishing holes.

Fortunately, some people are helping this snake. They don't release new crayfish into streams and keep cattle from trampling on stream banks.

To help protect garter snakes, you can provide good habitats for snakes around your home. Leave tall grass by streams, ponds, and ditches for garters to hide in while hunting. Keep pet cats indoors. These predators kill hundreds of garter snakes.

Remember that wild snakes are not meant to be pets. Many people catch garter snakes and keep them in cages. The snakes may even become tame and gentle when handled regularly. But pet snakes are often fed the wrong types of food. Some snakes don't get enough water or are kept in cages that are not warm enough. Many pet snakes die.

If you find a snake in nature, watch it without picking it up. The best way to protect snakes is to just let them be.

GLOSSARY

adaptation (a-dap-TAY-shuhn)—a change a living thing goes through to better fit in with its environment

cold-blooded (KOHLD-BLUH-duhd)—having a body temperature that changes with the surroundings

enzyme (EN-zime)—a substance that helps break down food

erosion (i-ROH-zhuhn)—a slow wearing away of soil by water or wind

habitat (HAB-uh-tat)—the natural place and conditions in which a plant or animal lives

hibernate (HYE-bur-nate)—to spend winter in a resting state to survive poor conditions in the environment

migrate (MYE-grate)—to move from one place to another when seasons change or when food is scarce

predator (PRED-uh-tur)—an animal that hunts other animals for food

prey (PRAY)—an animal hunted by another animal for food

reptile (REP-tile)—a cold-blooded animal that breathes air and has a backbone; most reptiles lay eggs and have scaly skin

species (SPEE-sheez)—a specific type of animal or plant

venomous (VEN-uh-muss)—able to produce a toxic substance

READ MORE

McDonald, Mary Ann. *Garter Snakes*. New Naturebooks. Chanhassen, Minn.: The Child's World, 2007.

Menon, Sujatha. *Discover Snakes*. Discover Animals. Berkeley Heights, N.J.: Enslow Publishers, 2009.

Stewart, Melissa. *Snakes!* National Geographic Readers. Washington, D.C.: National Geographic, 2009.

INTERNET SITES

FactHound offers a safe, fun way to find Internet sites related to this book. All of the sites on FactHound have been researched by our staff.

Here's all you do:

Visit *www.facthound.com*

Type in this code: 9781429654333

INDEX